A Note to Parents & Teachers—

Welcome to I See Trucks from Xist Publishing! These books are designed to inspire discovery and delight in the youngest readers. Each book features very simple sentences with visual cues to help beginners read their very first text.

You can help each child develop a lifetime love of reading right from the very start. Here are some ways to help a beginning reader get going:

- Read the book aloud as a first introduction
- Run your fingers below the words as you read each line
- Give the child the chance to finish the sentences or read repeating words while you read the rest.
- Encourage the child to read aloud every day!

Copyright © Xist Publishing 2025
First Edition
All Rights Reserved.
No portion of this book may be reproduced without express permission from the publisher.

Published proudly in the State of Texas, USA by Xist Publishing
www.xistpublishing.com
24200 Southwest Freeway Suite 402- 290 Rosenberg, TX 77471
All images licensed from Adobe Stock
First Edition

Hardcover ISBN: 978-1-5324-5457-8
Saddle Stitch ISBN: 978-15324-5557-5
Perfect Bound ISBN: 978-1-5324-5458-5
eISBN: 978-1-5324-5456-1

I See Trucks
Delivery Truck

written by **August Hoeft**

xist Publishing
INSPIRING DISCOVERY & DELIGHT

2

I see a delivery truck.

3

The delivery truck is white.

The delivery truck has a lift gate.

7

The delivery truck holds boxes.

9

The delivery truck helps bring things.

10

11

I see a delivery truck.

Things to do next!

Write a Sentence

I see a _____.

Drawing

Make a drawing of your favorite truck.

Sharing

Talk to your classmates about your favorite picture in this book. Explain to them why you like it.

WORD LIST

a	I
boxes	is
bring	lift
delivery	see
gate	the
has	things
helps	truck
holds	white